MW01520607

The Little Book Of T-Shirt Ideas

Proven Formulas & Frameworks To Help You Generate Original Ideas Fast

© 2019 by Michael Essek

For permissions contact:

michael@michaelessek.com

Michael Essek

michael@michaelessek.com

www.michaelessek.com

The Little Book Of T-Shirt Ideas

Proven Formulas & Frameworks To Help You
Generate Original Ideas Fast

Michael Essek

Table Of Contents

Introduction

Do you struggle to come up with T-Shirt ideas?

In the past few years the Print-On-Demand T-Shirt industry has exploded - opening up thousands of new markets for T-Shirt designers and sellers alike.

Those new markets have made it possible for artists and illustrators - like myself - to make a full-time income from our art online.

But in order to make the sales required to generate that income, a designer needs a large and growing portfolio of work.

When I first started creating designs for T-Shirts and posting them online, I could not have imagined creating *hundreds*, much less *thousands* of designs.

Every design I created took me hours, and a fair amount of thought and effort went into each one.

It took me years to reach one hundred unique designs - but it wasn't until I reached around 300 that I saw my t-shirt royalty income begin to get close to my full-time job income.

So here's the lesson: If you want to make a sustainable, recurring income from your T-Shirt designs, then having a large portfolio is a minimum requirement.

But - in order to create lots of T-Shirt designs, you must first have a lot of T-Shirt *ideas*.

What Is A T-Shirt Idea?

Put simply, a T-Shirt Idea is a concept for a T-Shirt design.

It could be a short funny phrase that becomes a simple 'text only' design.

Or it could be a visual joke that requires a detailed and well thought out illustration.

Either way - every T-Shirt design starts out as an idea.

And the more ideas you have, the more designs you can ultimately create.

Ideas Are Not Magic

It often seems that certain people are gifted with the 'idea' gene - they are able to come up with incredible, original and unique ideas at the drop of a hat.

But it is my conviction that ideas are not magic - and that anyone who maintains a decent and sustained income from their ideas (and creative work) almost certainly has systems and processes in place that help them generate those ideas. (Whether they know it or not).

In other words, ideas have become something they do as a matter of habit - a process they engage in regularly just like any other repeatable process.

This was the case with myself.

When I eventually quit my job to work on T-Shirts full-time, I knew that my income was going to be largely based on the size of my portfolio - and that to increase my portfolio I needed to generate a lot of designs, and therefore a lot of ideas.

So I set myself the goal of generating 40 original ideas a week, usually leading to around 30 new T-Shirt designs weekly.

I would start my week with the 'idea generating' process - opening up my note taking app (Evernote) and jotting down ideas until I had reached my goal.

After a while I began to see that there were certain methods I repeatedly turned to, to help me generate ideas. Certain websites, certain formulas, certain processes kept popping up again and again.

As I honed these methods and began writing and eventually teaching others, it became clear that there were designers like me who didn't know or use the same methods I did, and they found my methods to be inspiring and helpful.

And so the idea behind this book was born - a quick-reference guide that could help anyone to generate lots of T-Shirt ideas by following a step-by-step process.

How To Use This Book

This book is intended as a practical 'how to' - that you can turn to whenever you need inspiration.

Each chapter contains a different T-Shirt idea framework or formula.

Each formula is explained, and a number of examples are provided.

Finally I give you a step-by-step technique to follow in order to generate a similar idea for your own market or niche, and an 'example workflow' that will illustrate exactly what I mean.

What This Book Will Not Do

This book is not going to help you with market or niche research.

Instead, this book assumes that you already have a particular market that you want to serve - or at least a subject or topic that you want to create ideas around.

(For example - almost all of the 'Example Workflows' in the book are based on the subject of 'Christmas').

Once you know your subject, your market or niche - you can turn to any chapter in this book and start generating original ideas straight away.

This book will help you generate ideas - but it will not do the thinking for you.

You must answer certain questions, solve certain problems and engage in brainstorming activities in order to give the formulas the 'inputs' required to work.

The better your knowledge of the market or subject - the higher the quality of your 'inputs' will be - and so the better the quality of your final ideas will be.

As the old saying goes - Garbage in, garbage out.

Useful Bits

Finally, this book contains almost everything you need to get started and dive in.

However, from time to time, and depending on the idea or formula, you may want to use external resources to help speed things up.

For example, to help find words that rhyme with my input words, I use Rhymezone.com

You may also find an online Thesaurus like Thesaurus.com helpful when trying to generate related input words or variations.

And the most often used tool in my arsenal is simply Google.com and Google.com/images - to help give me inspiration and deliver subjects or topics related to my niche/market.

If you make use of all these free tools, then idea generation will become even easier.

—

Now that you know what T-Shirt ideas *are*, what this book is *for*, and how to use it - it's time to get started!

It's my hope that using this book will make you a more productive, creative and original idea generator - and lead you to create succesful T-Shirt designs in the weeks, months and years to come.

Enjoy!

- *Michael Essek*

5 Things I've Learnt About Idea Generation

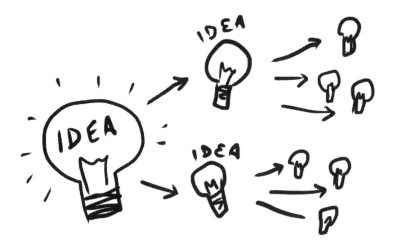

In the past 5 years I have generated thousands of ideas - many of which never saw the light of day as actual, created T-Shirt designs.

In that time I've honed my methods and learnt a lot about what works and what doesn't.

In this chapter I'm going to lay out some of what I've gathered over that time - and I'm sure this advice will help you as you become your own ideas generating machine.

1. Lots Of Ideas Leads To Good Ideas

"The best way to have a good idea is to have lots of ideas."

— Linus Pauling

When creating original work and trying to sell it in some form - and especially when relying on organic traffic to drive sales - it often seems like there is very little rhyme or reason to what actually 'hits'.

You can create 10 original designs - but only 2 will become good sellers, 2 will sell occasionally, and the remaining 6 will sell very rarely (for example).

There are of course reasons why popular designs become popular - but it's often hard to see, discern or apply these reasons from the other side of the creative process.

When you sit down to create, you simply can't be sure what's going to work - and so you must create in order to to explore and discover what will 'hit'.

And it's very hard to discover a winning design if you have only a small number of ideas.

The quickest way to find a winning design is to create a *lot* of designs - because the more designs you create - the greater that chances will be that one of them is a winner.

I'm not saying you should pursue volume above all else - but most designers - and especially beginners - vastly underestimate the amount of work and effort required to actually begin to see some movement and some sales.

You can't get a decent estimate of your earnings potential if you only have 10 designs up.

So, for a while at least, grab the bull by the horns and simply dedicate yourself to the task of creation - first by generating as many unique, original ideas as possible, and then by filtering those to find the best and strongest amongst them.

If you don't think you are coming up with *any* good ideas - it's probably because you aren't coming up with *enough* ideas.

2. Ideas Beget Ideas

Every idea is like a rabbit hole, with near endless possibilities to explore.

Don't think of an idea as some complete unit - but instead understand that ideas are composites of different elements (jokes, contrasts, formulas) - and each of those elements can be explored and extended and can lead to more and more ideas.

Ideas lead to ideas, if you let them.

Once you have a single funny idea, you can almost certainly extend it to find other ideas on the same subject, or based on the same underlying joke.

Consider the following example:

"Ghouls Just Wanna Have Fun"

This is a pun that works because of the similar sounds of the words 'Ghouls' and 'Girls'.

Once you have an idea like this, you can keep running with it.

You can look for other idioms and phrases that contain the word 'Girls' - and likewise replace them with 'Ghouls'.

For example;

- *Girls Night Out / Ghouls Night Out*
- *School For Girls / School For Ghouls*
- *A Big Girls Blouse / A Big Ghouls Blouse*
- *Cowgirl / CowGhoul*

...and so on.

That's just one framework (a 'classic' pun) - but the same system works with almost every repeatable framework you could find (it might just take a bit more work to figure out the ingredients).

The important thing is to let your mind wander - to follow the rabbit hole wherever it goes - and to not simply 'stop' at the first idea that pops into your head.

It's often when you force yourself to push an idea further and farther that you will hit a 'gusher' - and then you'll be able to list out 10, 20 or 30 ideas all from the same underlying principle or joke.

3. Ideas Can Always Be Improved

Just because you had a great idea doesn't mean it's finished.

Of course every idea must be turned into an appropriate design - and that takes time and effort.

But even before the design stage, it often helps to spend time working and re-working an idea - to ensure you've squeezed every possible angle out of it.

Consider especially how you are going to 'present' your idea - as a final design.

There's often several ways of doing so, and this process can spark new points of view that could in fact change or improve the nature of your original idea (or lead to entirely new ideas).

There's been many instances where I had an idea, quickly rushed out a design, and then weeks or months later discovered that there was an obvious improvement I could have made to either the joke, the text, or the design itself.

With a little more thought and a little less speed, I could have caught those opportunities sooner, and created just one killer design, rather than one mediocre one first.

Here's what to look out for;

- **Phrasing.** Don't be afraid to try variations and alterations to the order of words in a sentence, or to the *choice* of words. Often making a simple change can mean the different between a snappy design and a cumbersome one.

- **Graphics.** There's more than one way to skin a cat. Just because you had an idea that came 'bundled' in your head with a particular illustration or subject, doesn't mean that it's the only one that will work. Does your phrase or joke work when applied to other objects, subjects or characters? There might be one such example that works even better.

- **Graphic Style.** The style of your idea may already be set in your head - but again it pays to consider alternatives. Perhaps you haven't yet thought about the 'style' at all. Is there a particular illustrative method that would really enhance your idea? It could be something that really 'fits' with the design - or alternatively something that really contrasts with it - adding to the joke.

Simply by spending a few extra minutes pondering these questions and jotting down alternatives and extensions to your idea could mean the different between 'just okay' and 'really really good idea'.

4. The More Levels, The Better

This follows on from the previous point - in that the more levels of meaning and humour you can apply to an idea and design - the better the outcome.

Consider the '*Ghouls Just Wanna Have Fun*' example.

Now this could work simply as a text-only design - a few lines of text on a shirt. *(Level 1)*.

To level it up - we would add some kind of graphic.

Maybe an illustration of a ghost. *(That's level 2).*

But to really make the most of the idea, we need another level.

So perhaps the ghost is dressed like Cindi Lauper - red hair, lipstick etc. *(Level 3).*

Finally you could top things off with an 80s style font and colours, to really tie the whole piece together. *(Level 4).*

When you spend some time thinking about how to 'level' up your idea - especially when it comes to the design side - you can take something from dull to poppin' with just a few quick tweaks.

5. An Idea Can Be Presented In Different Ways

Sticking with our '*Ghouls Just Wanna Have Fun*' example - let's look at the different ways to present this idea.

We've already covered the 'levels'; from a simple text-only design to a detailed illustration.

But what about the *nature* of that illustration - or the style?

The underlying contrast between two things (Ghouls/Girls) - can also apply to the nature of our graphics and their style.

On one hand we have the Cindi Lauper, 80s-style driven graphics (bright neon colours, retro fonts, background squiggles and shapes etc.)

But on the other hand we have the 'Ghouls' side *(the other 'thing' that creates the joke)* - and this could lead us down a more ghost, horror or halloween-led graphic style.

For example, instead of 80s style graphics, we could use a vintage horror movie poster style - with a red, bloody font for the text, a haunted house, and a creepy zombie illustration.

In other words - whenever you have a joke or pun of this nature - there's almost always going to be an obvious 'alternative' way of spinning the idea - based on the style and nature of the graphics.

Now you might decide that the 80s version leads to a funnier and more easily understandable design (I think that's true in this case) - but it doesn't hurt to explore the 'opposite' approach when you are going from idea to concept to design.

—

So there you have it - 5 big things I've learnt that you can apply to your idea generation process - in order to help you 'level up' in more ways than one.

Put these tidbits to work in your business and watch yourself go from idea zero to idea hero!

The Idea Process

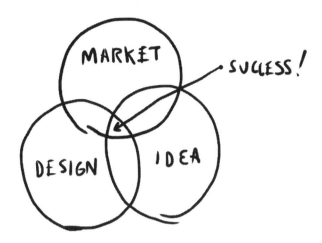

T-Shirt ideas are obviously important - they're the first step in any successful T-Shirt design.

But ideas are just part of a much bigger picture - a larger process that must take place if you're going to have any level of success.

In this chapter I'm going to walkthrough that process, and talk about the other major elements that must be in place if you want to see good results from your good ideas.

The Market

No T-Shirt idea ever turns into sales unless there is a market for that idea and design.

What do I mean by market?

Put simply, it's *'the people who would buy this Shirt'*.

If nobody wants to buy what you create, then you will never make a sale.

To illustrate, I'm going to describe a 'perfect' T-Shirt market scenario. In this scenario you would be almost 100% certain to generate sales if you just did the obvious - because you have a near perfect 'market' to sell to.

The Perfect Market Scenario

Let's say that one day you wake up to an email from a well-known online influencer. Could be a youtuber, a gamer, a musician or whatever. But this person has a huge online following.

The influencer emails you and says they have seen your design work, and they would like to commission you to create a design for their next T-Shirt release. Furthermore they want to split the earnings with you from all sales.

Whatever you create, the influencer is going to list it on their website, wear it every day for a month, and advertise the design on all their social media channels (pushing people to buy it day after day after day).

That's what you might call an 'ideal market' situation.

You really don't even need to have a great idea or even a great design - because the influence of this individual is going to result in sales regardless.

There are simply *so many people who would buy the Shirt*, that you are almost certain to generate sales.

Now of course this scenario is unlikely to happen, but I use it to illustrate the concept of a *market*.

Those people who would buy that shirt - they are the *market*.

You may not ever have access to such a large and accessible market as in this example - but you must tap into *some* kind of market - *some* group of people likely to purchase your Shirts. Otherwise you are unlikely to ever make sales.

Defining Your Market

The market you are trying to reach with your design could be anything from '*Democrats*' to '*6 year old boys who love squirrels*'.

But you *should* be able to explain - in just a few words or a few sentences - who you see as the likely buyers of your design.

If you have no idea who might buy your Shirt, then you have a problem.

If you already have an idea or design in the works, but you aren't clear about the market that such an idea would sell to - here's some questions you can ask to help you:

- What is the subject/topic of my design / idea?
- (If no obvious subject) What are the elements or illustrations?

- Does this subject have a following of some kind?
- How would I describe a group of people interested in this subject?
- If a person was interested in this subject, what else are they interested in?
- In what 'category' might I place the subject of my idea?
- What groups of people would recognise and 'get' my idea?
- Where (what stores) might such an idea be found on the shelves?

Once you have a clear picture of your market, you can make informed and intelligent decisions about the nature of your design; the idea, the content, the style, the colours, the fonts and so much more.

Alternative Markets

Not all markets are driven or defined by demographics or occupation.

For example, there exists such a thing as the 'Funny T-Shirt' market.

This spans demographics, and isn't limited to any particular age group, occupation or location.

So it's perfectly possible to design Shirts for the 'Funny T-Shirt' market. But you must also know how and where you are going to reach said market, if you want to be succesful and make sales.

Another example is the 'Aesthetic T-Shirt' market.

People looking for a Funny T-Shirt are unlikely to be hanging out in the same places as people looking for an Aesthetic T-Shirt.

You need to know the market you are trying to reach so that you can make good decisions about the nature of your designs, and about how you will get your work in front of the right people.

Not All Markets Are Equal

It's worth pointing out that *knowing* your market is not - on it's own - a guarantee of sales.

Many markets are saturated or highly competitive.

Some markets are so small that it's difficult to reach enough people to ever make a sale.

So it's not enough to just know the market you want to enter - you must also be able to get eyeballs on your work within that market -and to do so profitably.

The Importance Of Design

Once you have a list of good ideas, the next step is to turn them into great designs.

I talked about that process in the previous chapter - but let's talk briefly about the importance of design within the bigger picture.

I don't believe there's any such thing as the 'perfect' T-Shirt design - or even the perfect design for any particular idea.

But I do believe there is such a thing as 'appropriate' and 'inappropriate' design.

For example - for a halloween design aimed at young children, an inappropriate design might include overtly detailed gory horror graphics.

Likewise, for a halloween design aimed at 40+ year old horror fanatics - you probably don't want to use toddler-friendly cartoon style graphics with rainbow colours.

The key point here is that any design you create should 'fit' with the market expectation - and there should be no disconnect between what a customer is expecting or hoping to see, and what they actually do see. *(Eg. A customer searching for a 'Che Guevara shirt' is most likely expecting to find the iconic portrait in black ink on a red Shirt - not a cartoon version of Che Guevara in full colour on a white shirt).*

So let this be the guiding principle when you are deciding on your design - does this 'fit' with what my customer is expecting? Why or why not?

To help you with these decisions you can simply search the internet for related terms + 'T-Shirt' - or for a phrase like 'T-Shirts for (X)' *(X being your target market)*.

If you find recurring styles of design (or recurring colours, font styles, subject matter etc) - and especially if you discover those designs are selling - then it would probably be foolish to ignore what you see and create something that is the exact opposite of that (unless you have a good reason - for example, irony).

Don't try to 'beat' the market - instead work with it and create something in line with what said market is likely to respond to.

Deploying To Your Market

Once you have good ideas, targeting a clear market, and then turned into appropriate designs - it's time to 'deploy' your designs so that they can start to make money for you.

This is the final piece of the puzzle, and it could take many forms.

For example;

- Uploading your design to a print-on-demand platform with organic traffic *(eg. Merch By Amazon, Redbubble, Teepublic).* If you are 'deploying' your design here - then you need to think about how you can best optimise your chances of being found - by using appropriate Titles, keywords and descriptive data.
- Listing it on a marketplace like Etsy.com - along with appropriate mockup images.
- Submitting your design to a competition site (eg. Threadless) or a Shirt-A-Day site (eg. Teefury, TheYetee).
- Listing the design on your own-brand Shopify store (or similar) - and driving traffic to it via social media or advertising.
- Adding your design to a collection that you present to potential licensing partners - either in person or online.

Regardless of where or how you deploy your designs - the objective is the same:

Get your design in front of people who are likely to purchase it.

If you have good market knowledge, and have produced an appropriate product (design) - then getting said product in front of your market is the last step on the journey.

And if, following deployment, you discover that your design is *not* generating sales, it means one of the following things is happening:

- There is no market for your design
- The market has not seen your design
- The market has seen your design but doesn't like it

If there is no market, then you should stop creating such designs.

If the market has not seen your design - then you need to figure out how to increase the chances of your design getting seen.

And If the market has seen your design but doesn't like it - then you need to work on your idea, or the appropriateness of your design.

—

OK - that's my walkthrough of Idea -> Deployment explained.

Hopefully this clears some things up for you and will give you some clarity and confidence as you go on to generate ideas and turn them into best-selling designs.

Now, let's get into the ideas!

Idea 1: This Is My (X) Shirt

This is a text-based, 'Classic' t-shirt phrase formula that works like a charm.

Some example concepts:

- **This Is My Camping Shirt**
- **This Is My Christmas T-Shirt**
- **This Is My Hangover T-Shirt**
- **This Is My Zombie Killing Shirt**

Why is the 'This Is My (X) Shirt' formula worth using?

- It's a recognisable 'classic' t-shirt slogan. That means people 'get the joke' with very little explanation needed. And because it's a classic - and therefore proven pattern - it's more likely to 'hit' than a random idea.
- It 'labels' the wearer. It makes a clear statement about who is wearing it, and what they are into.
- It's a statement shirt - meaning it assumes or initiates a conversation or interaction between wearer and observer. That gives the shirt an extra dimension and a hook.

How To Use This Formula

Start with a topic, trend or market and see what related ideas or words would fit, using the 'This Is My (X) Shirt' formula.

Ask questions like;

- If a person from **Your Target Market** was wearing a 'This Is My (X) Shirt' - what would (X) be?
- What activities or actions *(e.g. drinking, camping, bowling, etc.)* would my target market engage in? *(And then simply replace (X) with your answer).*

Example Workflow:

Topic: *Christmas*

(Christmas) related activities or actions: *Drinking Eggnog, Wrapping Presents, Decorating The Tree, Carving The Turkey, Eating Brussel Sprouts, Passing Out After Dinner, Getting Into An Enormous Family Row, Crying In The Bathroom…etc.*

Example Results:

- *This Is My Eggnog Drinking Shirt*
- *This Is My Gift Wrapping Shirt*
- *This Is My Tree Decorating Shirt*
- *This Is My Turkey Carving Shirt*
- *This Is My Enormous Festive Family Row Shirt*
- *This Is My Crying In The Bathroom Shirt*

(All that's left is for you to add your festive graphics, ugly Christmas Sweater style elements etc.)

FOR EXTRA CREDIT:

See if you can apply some visual element - or trick - or *twist* - that will give your concept a further dimension.

For Example:

- This Is My Handstand T-Shirt *(with text upside down)*
- This Is My Zombie Killing T-Shirt *(complete with blood splatters)*

- This Is My Selfie Shirt *(with text mirrored/reflected for selfies)*

Idea 2: (X) Gang

This is a super-simple concept, but it has almost endless variations - and so can lead to a lot of unique ideas.

The idea here is simply to label the wearer as belonging to a certain group, gang, club or tribe of some kind.

People love to identify themselves as members of some kind of organisation (real or not) - and every gang needs a gang T-Shirt featuring the gang logo.

Examples:

- **Black Coffee Drinkers Club**
- **Girl Gang**
- **Unicorn Squad**
- **Proud Member Of The Basket Of Deplorables**

Why Is The (X) Gang formula worth using?

- It's a standard shirt format that makes sense to wearer and observer alike. Very little explanation needed.
- It makes a statement of affiliation and 'labels' the wearer.
- It's very easy to adapt to any topic or trend…because there are many different ways of saying 'club'. And those many ways can incorporate extra levels of humour - eg. Alliteration, rhyming, puns and juxtaposition.

How To Use This Formula

1. Start with your topic, trend or market - and list out potential words that would make sense to that market. Ask questions like: *what words are associated with my target market?*
2. Take your list and compare it to a list of synonyms for a word like 'club' or 'gang' *(see URL provided below)*
3. Run through your list of words and compare it to the synonyms - to see if there are any that work together *(either as rhymes or as alliteration, or just as a pleasant phrase).*

Example Workflow:

Topic: *Gardening*

List of related words: *flowers, plants, ho, pots, tomatoes, vegetables, dirt, cactus, succulents, landscaping.*

Synonym list: *https://www.thesaurus.com/browse/gang*

Results:

- *Gardening Gang*
- *Flower Family (or Flower Fam)*
- *Plant Posse*
- *Pot Pack*
- *Tomato Troop*
- *Cactus Crew*
- *Succulents Squad*
- *Landscapers League*

As you can see with these examples - I've gone down the alliteration route *(words that start with the same letters or sounds)* - as that's often something that works well.

But if you can find a pair of words that rhyme, even better.

EXTRA CREDIT:

Adding additional text or context can really take things up a notch.

For example, you could try adding extra bits like:

- Property of...
- Proud Member of...
- I'm In The...
- Join Your Local...
- ...Est. 1895 *(to give it an extra authenticity - as though your 'gang' were a real organisation)*
- ...San Diego, California *(as above)*

Idea 3: The 'Collection Of Things'

This is our first non-text-based idea - it's more of a 'visual framework'.

The idea here is that you find some way of displaying a 'collection of things' that are related to your topic or trend - ie. several different illustrations or graphics laid out together in a single design.

Why Is The 'Collection Of Things' Framework worth using?

Great question!

A 'Collection Of Things' design works great for a number of reasons;

- It makes for a more interesting and engaging design than a standard pun joke or single illustration. There's more to see, more to enjoy, more potential for laughs.
- It removes the pressure of having one single 'killer' illustration in your design that must do all the work. For example - a single Sexy Santa illustration may make for a good design. But by adding in several more Sexy Santa's in different poses - it takes the whole thing up a notch - and none of the individual illustrations have to be standalone awesome.
- A 'collection of things' design, whilst making for a great, high quality shirt piece - also MAKE SENSE on other products too: like posters, prints and journals. *(Whereas most standard shirt designs aren't going to make sense, or be especially appealing as posters, for example).*

How To Use This Framework

1. Starting with your topic, list out ideas for things you could illustrate, related to your topic. *(Think especially about; characters, objects, animals, food, plants - even things like situations or scenes.)*
2. Taking your list of potential illustration subjects - think about how you could throw these things together to form a 'collection' of some kind.

To short cut this part, here's a few 'tried and true' patterns:

- A-Z of (X) *(eg. Different things beginning with different letters.)*
- (X) In Different Poses *(eg. A character in different poses or settings.)*
- Several Different Versions of (X) *(eg. A single concept - like geometric butterflies - but with more than one version)*

Example Workflow

Topic: *Christmas*

List of things we could illustrate: Christmas characters *(snowmen, Santa, elves, reindeer, etc.)*, Christmas food *(turkey, Christmas pudding, gingerbread men, Brussel sprouts)*, Christmas scenes *(drinking cocoa in front of the fire, decorating the tree, carving the turkey, opening presents)*, Christmas objects / items *(stars, snowflakes, decorations, wreaths, ice skates, hats and scarves - etc.)*

Idea Results:

- (A collection of) Elves doing different dance moves (poses)
- (A collection of) Christmas Foods In a 3 x 3 grid (illustrated in your style)
- (A collection of) Several Illustrations of A Snowman in different Christmas scenarios - drinking cocoa, decorating the tree etc.
- (A collection of) various Christmas decorations forming an interlocking pattern.
- A Cartoon Christmas Pudding doing different Christmas Activities - ice skating, snowboarding, carving the turkey etc.

- 'A-Z of Christmas' - Christmas objects beginning with each letter of the alphabet

...as you can see, it doesn't take a lot to get the ideas flowing.

By starting out with just a simple subject (Christmas) and a tried-and-true framework ('collection of things') - we force our brains to find ways of working the two things together - hopefully in some funny and original ways.

Idea 4: Less (X), More (X)

Need a smart snappy phrase that really 'pops'? This framework ticks all the boxes.

Examples:

- **Less People, More Cats**
- **Less Talk, More Chalk**
- **Less Mondays, More Coffee**
- **More Espresso, Less Depresso**

Why Is The 'Less (X), More (X)' Framework Worth Using?

- It makes for a really simple, pithy phrase. which is perfect for T-Shirts - which often need to be quickly read and easily understood.
- It usually plays on an 'Us vs. Them' narrative, which is present in a lot of markets. *(eg. Vegans vs. Meat-eaters, Republicans vs. Democrats etc.)*
- It's another strong 'statement' framework - identifying the wearer as holding to a particular position, and initiating some form of interaction between wearer and observer.

How To Use This Formula

1. Starting with your subject, topic or market in mind - list out associated concepts, activities or nouns.
2. Identify potential rhyming pairs that also contrast in some way with your initial word.
3. Simply slip your contrasting & rhyming words into the 'Less (X), More (X)' framework

Example Workflow:

Topic: *Christmas*

Associated concepts, activities, nouns: *cheer, joy, peace, family, presents, gifts, snow, snowmen, elves, cold, ice, skating, gift wrapping, decorating, gingerbread, mince pies, Christmas lights, snowflakes...*

Rhyming opposites / contrasts:

- cheer / fear
- presents / antidepressants
- gifts / rifts
- elf / self
- ice / spice
- skating / hating
- skating / waiting
- wrapping / napping
- pies / sighs
- lights / fights
- snowflake / fake

Results:

- *Less Fear, More Cheer*
- *Less Antidepressants, More Presents*
- *Less Rifts, More Gifts*
- *Less Self, More Elf*
- *More Spice, Less Ice*
- *Less Hatin', More Skatin'*
- *Less Waiting, More Skating*
- *Less Gift Wrapping, More Christmas Nappin'*

- *Less Sighs, More Mince Pies*
- *More Christmas Lights, Less Christmas Fights*
- *More Snowflakes, Less Fakes*

...piece of Christmas cake, right?

Further tips:

- Your 'opposites' or 'contrasts' don't have to rhyme, but rhyming pairs often produce the pithiest of phrases, and therefore the best results. Alliteration may also work well, but sometime you won't need either rhyming or alliteration at all. *(eg. 'Less People, More Cats')*
- Reverse the order of 'Less' and 'More' - this could create a better phrase *(eg. 'More Espresso, Less Depresso')*
- Append additional words to extend your phrases. They don't always have to be single word opposites. *(eg. 'Less Christmas Fights, More Christmas Lights')*
- If you find rhyming pairs that don't exactly contrast, you can just replace the 'More/Less' framework with an 'AND'. *(Eg. 'Clear Skies AND Mince Pies')*

Idea 5: The Fake Pocket

Another fun visual-driven idea here - and again this one is super simple.

Take something (or someone) - stick them in a mocked up pocket - and voilà - you're done!

Examples:

- **Pomeranian in My Pocket**
- **Chipmunks In My Pocket**

- **Sun In My Pocket**
- **Christmas Corgi In Your Pocket**

Why Is The '(Fake) Pocket' Framework Worth Using?

- It gives the impression that the wearer is carrying something (or someone) in their pocket - and people love that 'real-world' effect. Especially effective for kids shirts.
- It's a subtle, visual way to indicate knowledge or appreciation towards something. *(as opposed to an overt 'I love Pomeranians' text based design)*
- Easy to execute - you can often use existing artwork and just make some minor tweaks.

How To Use This Formula

1. You need a 'subject'. ideal subjects are characters, animals, individuals (people) and ideally things that are small or pocket sized in real life (rabbits, kittens, cute animals etc.).
2. Once you have your 'subject' (animal / character etc.) - simply sketch them out inside a transparent pocket.

The most important thing here is to pick a good subject - something that 'works' and 'appeals' to your target audience. 'Cute characters' *(of some flavour)* is usually the order of the day.

Example Workflow:

Topic: *Christmas*

Possible Subjects: *Santa, Elves, Snowmen, Reindeer, nutcracker, penguin, gingerbread man. anthropomorphised objects like: a christmas pudding, christmas tree, baubles, christmas gifts etc.*

Results:

- *Santa in a pocket*
- *Elf in a pocket (or elves)*
- *Snowman in pocket*
- *(Baby) Reindeer in pocket*
- *Nutcracker in pocket*
- *Gingerbread man in pocket*
- *Christmas pudding (cartoon style, with face, christmas hat etc.) in pocket, (or tree, baubles, gifts .etc)*

Further tips:

- For extra credit, have a think if there's anything you could add that would 'take it up a notch'. eg. if your animal has a tail, you could poke a hole in the pocket and have the tail sticking out. or you could add multiple characters.
- If your subject isn't a naturally small animal, you could illustrate as a baby version instead *(extra cute points!)*
- You may want to be explicit in your listing data *(description text)* that the 'pocket' in the design isn't real, and is just printed onto the

design. I have had the occasional negative review from buyers who assumed the pocket was actually real.

- Get your positioning right! artwork should be right at the top of your canvas, and usually as far to the right as possible.

Idea 6: (X) Is My (X)

Today's idea is a text-based formula that helps to create original, funny phrases.

Examples:

- **Coffee Is My Spirit Animal**
- **Shopping Is My Cardio**
- **Dirt Is My Glitter**
- **Baking Is My Superpower**

Why Is The '(X) Is My (X)' Framework Worth Using?

- It's a cooler, smarter and wittier way of saying "I like (X)"
- It compares and contrasts the given interest or activity against something else - creating a joke in-and-of itself. *(because everyone knows - for example - that shopping is not really exercise)*
- It's another strong statement framework that identifies the wearer and can spark conversation.
- There's the opportunity to make things 'extra' funny - by making the compared 'thing' (the second 'X') - some obscure reference that only those 'in the know' would get. *(eg. 'X is My Patronus').*

How To Use This Formula

1. You will need an interest, activity, skill or noun that is familiar to your target audience, or market. (so make a list)

If you're struggling to come up with ideas for the above - simply imagine yourself in the mind of your target market, and complete sentences like:

- "I Like (X)"
- "I'm into (X)"
- "I really like to (X)"

...and your X's will become your list of things.

2. Compare your list of 'things' with the standard 'endings' of the '*(X) Is My (X)*' formula - and see if any ideas jump out.

Example Workflow:

Topic: *Christmas*

Interests/activities/skills/nouns: *drinking egg nog, decorating the tree, riding in a sleigh, wrapping presents, ice skating, singing carols, eating christmas pudding...santa, snowmen, elves, krampus, etc.*

Results:

- *Eggnog is my Spirit Animal*
- *Wrapping Presents is my Superpower*
- *Decorating the Tree is my Cardio*
- *Krampus is my Spirit Animal*
- *Christmas Pudding is my Spirit Animal*
- *Riding in a One Horse Open Sleigh is my Exercise*

Further tips:

- For more ideas, just google go-to phrases in this framework *(eg. 'spirit animal t-shirt', 'my cardio t-shirt')* - and try to analyse the jokes, and figure out why it works for that market.
- Make a list of all the '*...is my...*' phrases that you see *(eg. '...is my cardio, ...is my spirit animal, ...is my superpower')* - because the

longer your list, the better your ideas are likely to be. I've only given you 5 or 6 examples here, but there's lots more out there.

Idea 7: (X) For President

Let's talk politics!

With this framework you try to fit a given subject into a '...For President' type design.

Examples:

- **Pop-Pop For President**
- **Giant Meteor 2016**
- **Bigfoot For President**

Why Is The '(X) For President' Framework Worth Using?

- Whenever elections roll around, T-Shirts are a standard means of showing support. so a '...For President' type design makes sense and 'fits' as a recognised t-shirt pattern.
- As people recognise 'for President' type designs - any non-political subject you use in this framework creates a contrast, and therefore makes it (at least potentially) funny.
- Elections are a recurring feature of modern western democracies (a little *too* recurring here in the UK right now) - which means the 'trend' of election-based shirts will repeat regularly - and at such times people often enjoy wearing joke shirts that imply support for absurd entities and non-existent candidates.

How To Use This Formula

1. You'll ideally want a character or individual of some kind for this to work best. So list out individuals/characters (real or imaginary) related to your trend, theme or subject.
2. Working down your list or characters, place their name in front of *"...For President"*
3. See if any 'jump out' or appear especially funny to you.

Example Workflow:

Topic: *Christmas*

Individuals/characters: *Santa, Rudolph, Frosty the Snowman, Mrs. Claus, Krampus, Jack Frost, Ebenezer Scrooge, Ghost Of Christmas Past/Present/Future...etc.*

Results:

* *Santa For President*
* *Frosty The Snowman For President*
* *Mrs. Claus For First Lady*
* *Krampus 2018*
* *Ebenezer Scrooge For Chancellor Of Her Majesty's Exchequer*
* *Rudolph For Chief Of Staff*

Further tips:

* Don't limit your ideas to '...for President'. There are various ways to approach the same idea - eg.
  - (X) 2020 (whatever year is relevant)
  - (X) For America
  - (X) For Congress
  - I'm With (X)
* Think about famous presidential campaign graphics that you can parody.
* Think about other elements you can add for an extra joke. eg. Presidential tickets and graphics often include President AND Vice

President candidates - so you could go with '**Santa / Rudolph 2020**' or something like that.

- They also often have catchphrases or taglines, eg. *'Make America Great Again'*. So you could play on that and add it on - eg. *'Make America Festive Again'*, *'Make America Believe Again'*... etc.

Idea 8: Ask Me About My (X)

A well worn, well-known T-Shirt phrase that can be applied to almost any subject, niche or market.

Examples:

- **Ask My About My Video Game Achievements**
- **Ask Me About My Foster Dog**
- **Ask Me About My Dinosaur Collection**

Why Is The 'Ask Me About My (X)' Framework Worth Using?

- People love to talk about the things they care about and things they have achieved - and this framework encourages them to do just that!
- It's a recognisable funny T-Shirt phrase - which means people should 'get' the joke without much effort.
- It's an explicit conversation starter, between wearer and observer.

How To Use This Formula

1. List out skills, activities, objects, causes or collections of things that are related to your subject.
2. Simply work down your list of ideas, appending each to the 'Ask Me About My...' framework.
3. Take note of anything that jumps out!

(Pro Tip: to help you with step 1 - ask this question: "What does my target audience LOVE to talk about?")

Example Workflow:

Topic: *Christmas*

Related objects, activities, skills, causes, collections of things:
Christmas Tree, Christmas Holiday Plans, Snowball Fights, Christmas Decoration, Wrapping Presents, Reindeers, Premature Christmas Decorating, Christmas Carols...

Results:

* *Ask Me About My Christmas Plans*
* *Ask Me About My Tree Decorating Skills*
* *Ask Me About My Snowball Fighting Skills*
* *Ask Me About My Present Wrapping Skills*
* *Ask Me About My Reindeers (or Reindeer Collection)*
* *Ask Me About My Opposition To Premature Christmas Decorating*
* *Ask Me About My One Horse Open Sleigh*
* *Ask Me What I Want For Christmas*
* *Ask Me Who's On My Naughty List (or Nice List)*

Further tips:

* For more ideas and inspiration - do a google search for *'ask me about my t-shirt'* - and take note of what follows the 'ask me about' part. *(In particular try to categorise what that 'X' is. Is it a skill, a cause, or something else entirely?)*
* Use standard variations to help you generate ideas - for example;
  - ask me about my X **collection**
  - ask my about my X **skills**
  - ask me about my X **plans**
  - ask me about my X **agenda**
  - Ask my about my X **Achievements**
  - etc.

- Try to think about jokes, tropes and memes related to your topic, and whether you can use those within this framework. *(For example - there is a recurring joke about Christmas decorations going up earlier every year - and this led me to the 'Ask Me About My Opposition To Premature Christmas Decorating' idea.)*

Idea 9: (X)...And All I Got Was This Lousy T-Shirt

Another well-known T-Shirt phrase that can be applied to almost any subject - and with plenty of room for fun variations and additions.

Examples:

- **It's My Birthday And All I Got Was This Lousy T-Shirt**
- **Retired And All I Got Was This Lousy T-Shirt**
- **I Beat Cancer And All I Got Was This Lousy T-Shirt**

Why Is The '(X)...And All I Got Was This Lousy T-Shirt' Framework Worth Using?

- Everybody knows the phrase and recognises it.
- It can often be a self-aware or 'meta' type of design.
- It can be applied to endless subjects, and expanded and inverted in fun ways.

How To Use This Formula

First - understand this: the 'funny' in this phrase is usually built on the the contrast between "something bad I went through / something I missed out on" and the low-value of a t-shirt.

In other words, *"My Parents Went To Hawaii And All I Got Was This Lousy T-Shirt"* is funny because Hawaii is nice - but I didn't get to go, and this t-shirt is not so nice.

So here's what you need to do:

1. Think about potential 'suffering' points, or 'things people miss out on' - related to your topic. (It could be from the perspective of your target customer - ideally the wearer - but could also be from the perspective of a topic-related character or individual - see workflow below).
2. Once you have some concepts, try to add them to the front of the phrase formula, and try to make it make sense and read well.

Example Workflow:

Topic: *Christmas*

Topic-related situations that cause people to suffer:

(from the wearers perspective):

- cooking Christmas dinner for a big family
- decorating the tree by yourself
- going Christmas shopping (actually leaving the house)
- enduring Christmas day with family you don't like
- listening to the same Christmas songs over and over
- just the entire Christmas period

OR:

(specific characters / individuals who suffered somehow, related to topic):

- Rudolph - led santa's sleigh through the fog
- Donkey - carried Mary to Bethlehem
- Innkeeper - provided shelter for the birth of the Son of God
- Three Kings - travelled far to bring gifts to Jesus

Results:

- *I decorated the Tree and all I got was this Lousy T-Shirt*
- *I had to spend Christmas with all of you and all I got was this Lousy T-Shirt*
- *I had to listen to Christmas Songs every day for a month and all I got was this Lousy T-Shirt*

- *I Survived Christmas And All I Got Was This Lousy T-Shirt*
- *I led Santa's Sleigh and all I got Was this Lousy T-Shirt (and a carrot)*
- *The Son of God was born in my stable and all I got was This Lousy T-Shirt*
- *I gave gold to the Son of God and all I got was this Lousy T-Shirt*
- *I single-handedly started Christmas and all I got was some Gold, Frankincense and Myrrh from three weird old dudes*

Further tips:

- If you're doing this from the perspective of a character (as opposed to the wearer) - then you'll probably want to include an illustration of that character in the design to help it make sense. (or not - maybe the wearer is playing the role of Innkeeper in their nativity play, and just wants a funny shirt to wear).
- It doesn't have to end with 'T-Shirt'. There may well be better suited objects to complete the framework in your case - eg: *"I pulled Santa's Sleigh All Night And All I Got Was A Lousy Carrot"*
- Take note of oft-used beginnings to such phrases, and use these as jumping off points to help spark ideas. eg:
  - I Beat (X)...
  - I Survived (X)...
  - I Turned (X)...
  - We Did (X)...
  - I Lost (X)...
  - It's My (X)....
  - etc.

Idea 10: Anatomy Of (X)

This is another visual-led idea framework.

The idea is to do a biology-diagram-style illustration of your subject, complete with (usually comical) feature points.

Why Is The 'Anatomy Of (X)' Framework Worth Using?

- It gives you lots of room for extra jokes (with the 'feature' bullet points)
- It gives an opportunity for detailed, quality visuals (eg. 'cross section' style stuff)
- It gives you more options for future use - because this kind of visual transfers well to other products - posters, journals..etc.

How To Use This Formula

1. You'll need a character, animal, object, map, or some such graphic. so make a list of possibilities related to your topic.
2. Working through your list, consider how you might produce a 'diagram' of your subject, highlighting various features as though a graphic in a biology text book.
3. Finally, brainstorm potential 'features' assigned to particular parts of your subject. (complete with line, pointing out where feature is located).

Example Workflow:

Topic: *Christmas*

Possible Characters, Objects, etc: *Santa, Rudolph, an Elf, Krampus, Christmas Tree, Gingerbread man.*

Results:

- *Anatomy of Santa*
- *Anatomy of Krampus*
- *Anatomy Of Rudolph*
- *Anatomy Of Gingerbread Man*

Further tips:

- Take a look at similar 'anatomy' designs to spark more ideas and approaches. Just google 'anatomy of t-shirt' and take a look at what comes up.
- Brainstorm ways you can add an extra dimension - either by changing the illustration style, or by 'niching down' on your subject. *(So instead of just 'Santa' - it could be an evil santa, a grumpy santa, a sleeping santa...etc.)*
- The illustration 'subject' doesn't have to be a person or animal. it could be something like a map, or an image of the brain. *(it's the same principle - a kind of diagram of a subject, but without the need for a character).*

Idea 11: I Survived (X)

A simple, text-based framework that works especially well for event-based ideas.

Examples:

- **I Survived My Trip To NYC**
- **I Survived The Wooden Spoon**
- **I Survived The Sixties (Twice!)**
- **I Survived Another Meeting That Could Have Been An Email**

Why Is The 'I Survived (X)' Framework Worth Using?

- It 'makes sense' as a kind of souvenir gift t-shirt - which adds to the humour
- The joke is 'built-in' to the phrase; because whatever you 'survived' is unlikely to have *actually* been dangerous (usually just inconvenient or annoying)
- It's super easy to use, and applicable in many different scenarios.

How To Use This Formula

1. You'll need events, scenarios, activities, situations and similar such subjects related to your topic. **(IMPORTANT: the more mundane and 'survivable' your event/situation - the better the joke)**
2. Simply append "I Survived..." to your given activity or event.
3. Take note of those that are especially funny or work well, and try to hone the sentence to make it read easier, and to make it as funny as possible.

Example Workflow:

Topic: *Christmas*

Related activities/scenes/scenarios: *Ice Skating, Christmas Tree Decorating, Christmas Dinner Preparation, After-Dinner Napping, Christmas Shopping, Christmas Office Party...etc.*

Results:

- *I Survived Christmas*
- *I Survived Christmas (w/ Illustration Of A Happy Turkey)*
- *I Survived Christmas 2018*
- *I Survived Decorating The Tree*
- *I Survived The Office Christmas Party, 2018*
- *I Survived The After Dinner Nap, Christmas 2018*
- *I Survived Christmas Shopping*
- *I Survived 2018*

Further tips:

- Think about how the use of images and graphics could enhance the joke. For example 'I Survived Christmas' is moderately funny, but it's funnier if you include an illustration of a Turkey giving a thumbs up, or wiping sweat from his brow.
- The addition of dates, years or similar specific details usually adds an extra element of humour.

Idea 12: The (Fake) Sports Team

Here's the deal - you invent a 'fake' sports team related to your topic, and create a logo for said team.

Some Examples:

- Tokyo Kaijus Baseball Team
- Fighting Cephalopods
- The Horizontal Running Team
- Rednecks (Redskins parody)

Why Is The '(Fake) Sports Team' Framework Worth Using?

- It's instantly recognisable as a design style, which means it looks like a 'real' sports team shirt (that's the joke)
- It implies membership or support of said 'team' - similar to the '(X) Gang' idea framework. And we know that people love to wear shirts that show their support for a sports team.
- It gives plenty of room for fun illustrations and related jokes (taglines etc.)
- It's readily transferable to other standard sports-related apparel products, such as hats, hoodies etc.

How To Use This Formula

Your 'Team Name' is going to follow the following formula:

The *(Location)* | *(Characters)*

For example:

- The Los Angeles Dodgers
- The Tokyo Kaijus

So here's what you need to do to make this happen:

1. With your topic in mind, brainstorm related characters, animals, groups or other 'sub-categories' that could be used as your 'Characters' phrase/word
2. Assuming you have some options there, you can move on to brainstorm potential 'Location' words - so look for related cities, towns, states, countries, continents, planets etc.

Then - Smash the two together!

If you're struggling to come up with potential 'Character' words - then take a look at this list of popular team 'names':
www.sportsfeelgoodstories.com/sports-team-names/

You can then use that list to help you brainstorm potential alliteration-based ideas, eg. 'The Wolverhampton Wanderers'. *(that one's not a joke).*

Example Workflow:

Topic: *Christmas*

Potential 'Characters': *Snowmen, Reindeers, Robins, Elves, Santas, Narwhals, Penguins, Puddings...*

Potential 'Locations': *The North Pole, Antarctica, Greenland...*

Resulting Ideas:

- *The North Pole Reindeers*
- *The Greenland Snowmen / Elves / Penguins (etc).*
- *Rudolph's Raiders*
- *The Christmas Cardinals*

- *Egg Nogg Eagles*
- *(Gift) Wrapping Warriors*

Get it?

All you need now is to use some typical sports-team-logo style fonts and associated graphics to tie the whole thing together.

Further tips:

- You can play off iconic sports logos and colours - but be careful to not use 'real' sports teams names or logos too closely (sports teams are typically very protective of their IP).
- Different sports and different countries have different team name conventions. For example, here in the UK, football teams use 'FC' (Football Club) - and usually use words like United, City, Wanderers, Rovers...etc.

Idea 13: Visit (X)

Everybody needs a summer vacation - but where to go?

This framework invites the viewer to visit your given location (fictional or not) - and imagines said location as a tourist hot spot.

Examples;

- **Visit Mordor**
- **Greetings From Skull Island**
- **Visit Mars**

Why Is The 'Visit (X)' Framework Worth Using?

- It gives plenty of room for quality visuals - and there are plenty of established graphic tropes you can rely upon. (eg. The 'vintage souvenir postcard' or the 'retro travel poster' style).
- Like other visual frameworks - this one lends itself to other products besides T-Shirts - posters, postcards, greetings cards etc.
- This is a recognisable T-Shirt format - that of the 'souvenir' Shirt. As such any non-real 'location' you use as the subject creates a conflict in the viewers mind, and produces the humour.

How To Use This Formula

1. You need a 'location' related to your subject. This location could be real, imaginary or abstract (for example: 'the couch').
2. Once you have a list of potential 'locations' - simply add 'Visit...' or 'Greetings From...' before your location name to create the basis of your design.
3. Complete the concept with appropriate (or inappropriate) graphics - such as a vintage tourist postcard style.

Top Tip: Your 'location' need not be an imaginary or fictional one in order to generate a funny design - 'real world' locations often have lots of potential for humour too.

For Example;

- "Visit Scotland - It's Wet"
- "Visit Beautiful Guantanamo Bay"
- "New Zealand....Rocks!!!"

Example Workflow:

Subject: *Christmas*

Possible Locations: *The North Pole, Greenland, Santa's Grotto, The Manger, Bethlehem, Santa's Workshop, A Winter Wonderland, The Roof, The Chimney, The Fireplace, Under The Tree*

Results:

- *Visit The North Pole*
- *Greetings From Greenland*
- *Visit Santa's Grotto*
- *Visit The Manger*
- *Greetings From Bethlehem*
- *Greetings From 'The Chimney' (when Santa got stuck)*

Further Tips:

If there are no obvious 'locations' related to your given subject - then you'll have to get creative.

Ask yourself questions like:

- If I had to draw (my subject) - where would the scene be set?

- If (my subject) owned it's own kingdom, it would be called 'the land of (x)' *(what's X?)*
- Can I relate my subject to any of the following concepts: a hotel? A theme park? A camp? A library? A museum? An island? A Festival? A park? A sea? A lake? A mountain? An area of natural beauty? A planet? An underground lair? An alternative dimension?

Using these prompts, you should be able to stimulate some ideas around potential 'locations'.

Idea 14: The Costume T-Shirt

Halloween rolls around once a year - and people need cheap costumes!

This visual-driven formula helps you to imagine potential 'costumes' related to your subject or topic.

Why Is The 'Costume T-Shirt' Framework Worth Using?

- It has that 'real world' element to it - making the design more than just a joke printed on a Shirt.
- It's perfect for occasions that call for fancy dress - whether that's Halloween or some other such event.
- It usually makes use of the T-Shirt colour itself - making for an aesthetically pleasing design.

How To Use This Formula

1. You need a list of related 'characters' that can serve as your subject matter.
2. Once you have a list of characters, make a note of those that have some kind of recognisable 'costume'.
3. Of those that are 'costume-able' - detail the elements that would need to be present in order for the design to work.

Example Workflow:

Subject: *Christmas*

Possible Characters: *Santa, Rudolph, Elves, Snowmen, The Three Kings, Shepherds, Angels, Krampus, Reindeers, Gingerbread Man, A Christmas Pudding*

Results:

- *Santa Costume T-Shirt (Red Shirt, White Trim and Black Belt)*
- *Reindeer Costume T-Shirt (Brown Shirt, Fluffy Brown Chest, Bells Around Neck)*
- *Snowman Costume T-Shirt (White Shirt, Black Coal Buttons)*
- *A Christmas Pudding Costume T-Shirt (Brown Shirt with White Cream, Possible Smiling Face - Perfect For Kids)*
- *GingerBread Man Costume T-Shirt (Brown Shirt, Gumdrop Buttons, Bowtie)*

Further Tips:

A lot of the obvious costume ideas will already be in play for major holidays - but that doesn't mean you can't use this framework by going deeper and adding another level.

Take the 'Santa Shirt' for example. How could you add another level to this? A drunk Santa? A tattooed Santa? Santa with his chest hair on display?

You get the idea.

Final Thoughts

Alright - you've seen all 14 Ideas!

What next?

Well just keep this book handy - and next time you need to generate some T-Shirt ideas, just pull it out, open it up - and generate away!

If you need a reminder of ideas then you can quickly glance at the sketches or examples to inspire you.

And if you want a more thorough reminder of how to enact these ideas for your subject or topic - turn to the 'How To Use...' and 'Example Workflow' sections.

Most importantly - let your brain run wild, and give yourself dedicated and focused time to generate original ideas.

Pretty soon you'll see some of these frameworks become 'second nature' to you - and generating ideas along those lines will be almost automatic.

But I Want More!

If you want more ideas, more help and more resources, be sure to join my newsletter at: *michaelessek.com/newsletter*

And you can find more products on my website here: *michaelessek.com/products*

Finally...

I hope you've enjoyed The Little Book Of T-Shirt Ideas - and I hope this guide will become a well-worn reference in your arsenal of tools.

My hope is that you'll use it to create hundreds of original, unique T-Shirt designs - and that it can form the basis of your creative-driven business for many years to come.

To Your T-Shirt Success!

Michael Essek

michaelessek.com

Notes

Notes

Notes

Notes

Notes

Notes

35562905R00054

Printed in Poland
by Amazon Fulfillment
Poland Sp. z o.o., Wrocław